The Mailbox

Written by Nicki Saltis

Illustrated by Bettina Guthridge

sundance

"I have something
from the mailbox,"
said Mom.

3

"Is it a bill?"
asked Dad.

"No. It's not a bill,"
said Mom.

"Is it a card?"
asked Sam.

"No. It's not a card,"
said Mom.

5

"Is it a newspaper?" asked Uncle Vin.

"No. It's not a newspaper," said Mom.

"Is it an invitation?"
asked Anna.

"No. It's not an invitation,"
said Mom.

7

"Is it a package?"
asked Sam.

"Yes. It's a package,"
said Mom.

"Is it for me?"
asked Sam.

"Yes. It's for you,"
said Mom.

"It's a present
from Grandma,"
said Sam.

"Yippee!"